The Brave Little Tailor
A Brothers Grimm Story

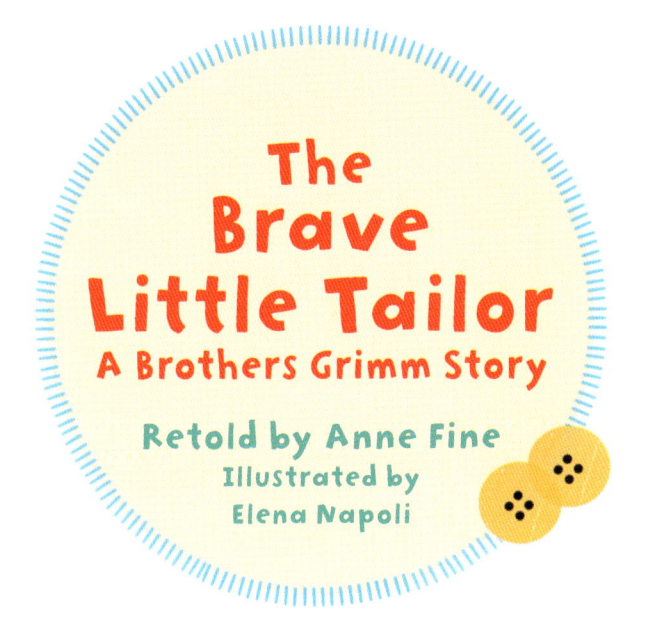

Retold by Anne Fine
Illustrated by Elena Napoli

Wilton Primary School
Burcombe Lane
Wilton
Salisbury
Wiltshire
SP2 0ES
01722 742621

RISING ★ STARS

ISBN: 9781510444348

Text © 2019 Anne Fine
Illustrations, design and layout © 2019 Rising Stars UK Ltd
First published in 2019 by Rising Stars UK Ltd

Rising Stars UK Ltd, part of Hodder Education Group
An Hachette UK Company
Carmelite House, 50 Victoria Embankment, London, EC4Y 0DZ

www.risingstars-uk.com

Impression number 10 9 8 7 6 5 4 3 2 1
Year 2023 2022 2021 2020 2019

Author: Anne Fine
Series Editor: Sasha Morton
Publisher: Helen Parker
Illustrator: Elena Napoli/Advocate Art
Cover illustrator: Tika and Tata/Bright Group International
Educational Consultant: Pauline Allen
Design concept: Helen Townson
Page layout: Steve Evans
Senior Editor: Kirsten Taylor

With thanks to the schools that took part in the development of *Reading Planet* KS2, including: Ancaster CE Primary School, Ancaster; Downsway Primary School, Reading; Ferry Lane Primary School, London; Foxborough Primary School, Slough; Griffin Park Primary School, Blackburn; St Barnabas CE First and Middle School, Pershore; Tranmoor Primary School, Doncaster; and Wilton CE Primary School, Wilton

All rights reserved. Apart from any use permitted under UK copyright law, no part of this publication may be reproduced or transmitted in any form or by any means, electronic or mechanical, including photocopying and recording, or held within any information storage and retrieval system, without permission in writing from the publisher or under licence from the Copyright Licensing Agency Limited. Further details of such licences (for reprographic reproduction) may be obtained from the Copyright Licensing Agency Limited, https://www.cla.co.uk/

A catalogue record for this title is available from the British Library

Printed in India

Orders: Please contact Bookpoint Ltd, 130 Park Drive, Milton Park, Abingdon, Oxon OX14 4SE.
Telephone: (44) 01235 400555. Email: primary@bookpoint.co.uk

Contents

Chapter 1 4

Chapter 2 8

Chapter 3 13

Chapter 4 17

Chapter 5 22

Chapter 6 25

Chapter 7 28

Chapter 1

Everyone in the village talked about the odd little tailor who sat in his workshop and sewed their new clothes, or mended their old ones. Was he as foolish as he seemed? The woman who went up and down the streets selling jam was sure he hadn't so much as a forkful of brain in his head.

"I asked him how many spoonfuls of jam he wanted me to put in his bowl," she told her friends. "Guess what he said! 'I'll have six spoonfuls. No! Change that to half a dozen!' How daft is that?"

They all agreed. "Truly, the little tailor is as silly as they come." And when they walked past his workshop a little later, they peeked through the window and saw him spreading the fresh jam thickly over a slice of bread.

He put the plate behind him, out of sight.

"That's not very clever," they whispered to one another. "How many flies will land on that jam before he turns to eat it?"

The answer was seven. When the tailor picked up the bread, he saw seven flies stuck in the jam, all struggling madly to get free.

The little tailor was furious.

"I'll teach you a lesson for ruining my bread and jam!" he cried. The tailor swung a length of cloth down on the bread as hard as he could, then took another look.

Now there were seven dead flies stuck in his jam.

Everyone outside waited to hear him complain about his spoiled snack, but he didn't. Instead, he looked delighted.

"Seven at one blow!" they heard him boasting to himself. "Seven! All at once! At one blow! Oh, I am one brave fellow."

The jam seller called through the window. "Seven dead flies? What's special about that?"

But the tailor wasn't listening. He had already pulled off his old leather belt and reached for his knife. "I'm going to let the whole world know about the amazing thing I've done," he said. "I'll carve the words that tell this wonderful tale into my belt so everyone will know how valiant I am. Seven at one blow!"

And that's what he did, while the village folk stood outside, watching and whispering.

"Not the brightest spark, is he?"

"Porridge for brains!"

"Can there be a bigger fool in the whole kingdom?"

When the tailor stepped out of his workshop, he threw his jacket open so everyone could read the words carved into his belt.

Seven at one blow!

And he wondered why everyone round him just hurried away, giggling.

Chapter 2

The tailor woke next morning and thought about his dull life. *I go to my workshop. I sit and sew all day. I come home and go to bed. I get up next morning and sit and sew all day – on and on.* He shook his head. *I should do better for myself. Why, a man as brave as I am, who can kill seven at one blow, should become a king and marry a princess. Yes! I will go into the world to seek my fortune.*

He dressed, strapped on his leather belt, and looked at himself in the mirror.

"Seven at one blow!" he read aloud.

"Strange," he declared. "I was quite sure I'd written *'Seven at one blow!'*"

Puzzled, he took off the belt and studied it. "Oh," he said after a moment. "I must simply have read it wrong." He strapped on the belt again, and opened his cupboard to find food for his journey.

The cupboard was almost bare. He'd eaten all his honey. He'd finished all his bread. The only food left on the shelf was a lump of soft cheese the size of his fist.

"Cheese is full of goodness," he told himself. "Eating this will keep me going over mountains and through forests."

He put the lump of cheese in his pocket and left the house. On his way to the gate, he heard a frantic rustling inside a nearby thorn bush. A little bird was trapped. Gently, the tailor freed her, but instead of letting her go, he stuffed her deep down in his other pocket, saying, "Stay there, little bird. You need to rest after all that struggling."

The poor bird now found herself not just trapped, but also in darkness. So, with her last hope gone, she gave up the struggle. The bird lay quietly in the little tailor's pocket while he set off to seek his fortune.

Was it the fresh air he drew into his lungs? Was it the way his legs felt stronger as he strode along? Something had filled the little tailor with confidence because when he came across a giant sitting on the most enormous log, he spoke to him bravely.

"Hey, Giant! I'm off to seek the fortune I deserve. Do you want to come with me?"

The giant stared. "With you? Why, you don't even come up to my knees! Why should a huge, strong giant like myself take up with a feeble, little squirt like you?"

The tailor scowled. "Feeble, indeed!" he cried. "I'll show you how strong I am." With that, he threw open his jacket to show the words carved on his belt.

Seven at one blow!

"My eyesight is poor," the giant admitted. "Come closer so I can see more clearly."

The little tailor stepped closer, and when the giant had read the words, he said, "You must have stolen that belt. Even I couldn't kill seven at one blow, and you can't be stronger than I am."

"I did kill seven at one blow," the tailor insisted.

"Then," said the giant, "you'll be able to do this!" And picking up the nearest fat, round stone, he squeezed it so hard that it crumbled into dust.

The little tailor remembered the lump of soft cheese in his pocket. "Now I shall need all the strength it can give me," he told himself, and pulled it out to eat it. But the cheese had been sitting in his pocket for so long that all the pale and watery whey dripped out of it, through his fingers and on to the ground.

The giant was astonished. His poor sight told him that the little tailor had pulled a stone from his pocket and was squeezing it so hard that water was dripping out of it.

"Why, I can scarcely believe my eyes," he said to the little tailor. "You certainly are a strong fellow."

But the tailor was even more astonished. "If I can surprise a giant, I must be even stronger than I thought!" he told himself.

And he felt even more confident than he had before.

Chapter 3

The giant was puzzled. The belt the little tailor wore boasted that he had killed seven at one blow. Still, the giant found it hard to believe.

"Your hands are strong," he admitted, "but maybe your arms are weak. Let's try a second trial of strength."

The giant picked up a stone and hurled it high in the air. Both of them stood and stared upwards for a count of a hundred before the stone at last came into sight again and fell to Earth.

The little tailor told himself, *If I can kill seven at one blow, and the giant can't, then surely I must be able to throw a stone higher than he can.*

To swing his arm more freely, he dug in his pocket to get rid of the bird that was still huddled there, making a lump against his side.

Seeing that her chance for freedom had come at last, the bird wriggled from his grasp and flew up, up and away. The giant, thinking she must be a stone thrown by the tailor, threw back his head to watch her go. He counted the moments – one hundred ... two hundred ... three ...

But the bird, of course, never came back.

The giant was astonished to find himself beaten in yet another test of strength. He insisted that the two of them undertake one last trial.

"Your hands are strong," he told the little tailor. "So are your arms. But what about the rest of your body? I challenge you to help me carry this oak tree I've uprooted down to the house where I live with my giant friend. We need the wood for our fire."

"Gladly," said the tailor.

The giant lifted the root end of the tree. "You hold the branches at the other end," he told the tailor. "Since I am the one who knows the way, I'll take the lead."

The little tailor reached down to lift a branch to do his share of the carrying. But then he thought to himself, *I have no need to prove my strength. I can kill seven at one blow, and the giant knows it. He is the one who wants the firewood. Why not let him do the work?*

So, the little tailor jumped on to the topmost branches and let the giant drag him all the way down the hill to his house. The tailor was perfectly confident that he could have carried the branches if he had wanted. The thought made him so happy that he whistled merrily all the way along the path, while the giant was huffing and puffing and complaining.

Only when they drew close to the massive front door of the giants' house did the tailor leap off and pretend to carry the branches again. "I feel as fresh as the morning dew," he told the giant. "But listen to you – moaning and groaning at the weight of a simple oak tree."

The giant was angry then, and muttered to himself, "Wait till night comes, my little man. However many you can kill at one blow when you're awake, my giant friend and I will have a nasty surprise for you when you're asleep!"

Then, stretching out a welcoming arm, he said, "Welcome to my home. Come in and meet my friend. He will be pleased to meet such a brave little tailor."

Happily, the tailor followed him into the enormous house.

Chapter 4

The tailor must have been very, very brave (or very, very foolish) because he did not feel in the least bit nervous when he walked through the door to find an even more enormous giant sitting beside the fire. His head was bigger than a pumpkin and his fists were as large as melons. As for his teeth – it would frighten me even to describe them!

The giant by the fire put down the roasted sheep bone he had been gnawing on, and stared at the tailor. "Who is this feeble-looking little fellow?" he demanded. "Have we now had enough of eating stolen sheep? Is he to be our supper?"

"No, indeed," said the first giant. "Why, this man here is the bravest you've ever met."

"Indeed I am," boasted the tailor. "I have killed seven at one blow!" And he opened his jacket to show the belt that made that splendid claim.

The second giant chuckled. "That I would dearly love to see!"

"Tomorrow will be soon enough," said the first giant. He blew on the fire till it blazed up, before hanging a massive pot of beans above the flames to warm. "First we will eat our supper and go to bed."

The tailor shared their supper, and since it had been a long day's journey for a little man, soon began yawning. The giants led him to a huge and gloomy room. "Be our guest here tonight," they told him. "Here is a bed for you."

Then, closing the door, they went back to the fireside. "Seven at one blow, indeed!" jeered the second giant. "But seven what, I ask you? Seven flies?"

The first giant wasn't so quick to mock the little tailor. "His hands are strong enough to squeeze water from a stone. His arms are strong enough to fling a stone so high it won't fall back to Earth. As for his body, that's strong enough to carry one end of an oak tree more than a mile."

His friend said fiercely, "Then we would be safer if he were gone forever!"

The two of them sat by the fire and plotted, while the little tailor tossed and turned on the enormous bed.

"I can't sleep here," he muttered. "I keep on worrying that I'll roll over the edge." He peered down nervously. "So far to fall!"

Taking one of the huge blankets, he slid off the bed and made a comfortable nest behind the door. There he slept soundly, not even waking when the giants crept in carrying enormous sheep bones, and pounded them on the bed.

"There!" said the first giant when they had beaten the covers into a crumpled heap. "That would be the end of any man, however many he can kill at one blow."

And they went off to bed to sleep till morning.

The giants were already away, deep in the forest, when the tailor awoke. "What an excellent night's sleep!" he said to himself.

He saw a huge bone lying on the bed he hadn't slept in. "Ah, breakfast!" he said, and chewed on it for a while. When he was no longer hungry, he followed one path after another, between the trees, to find his new companions.

At last, he came across the two giants, who were pulling great oak trees out of the ground to use as firewood.

The little tailor called out cheerily, "Good morning to you, my fine friends!"

In sheer astonishment, the giants dropped the trees they were holding. "Can this be true?" cried the first.

"Impossible!" cried the second.

The little tailor stepped closer. "Oh, I have had the most restful night," he told them. "Nothing disturbed my sleep, and I have woken feeling fresh and strong. I'm more than ready to show you both how I can kill seven at one blow."

Hearing this, the giants looked at one another in horror, then turned and fled. They ran deeper and deeper into the forest, hoping the little man who terrified them so much would never catch up with them.

The tailor tried to follow them. Down path after path he went, but soon he was so lost he gave up, and simply wandered along any forest track that took his fancy.

Suddenly, he found himself stepping out of the shadow of trees into sunlight. In front of him, there stood a shining palace with towers and parapets and fluttering flags.

"Now that," said the little tailor to himself, "would be a far more fitting home for me than my old cottage. After all, I can kill seven at one blow."

And he set off at once, across the fields towards the palace.

Chapter 5

High up in one of the palace towers, the king was grumbling to his daughter, as usual.

"You are my only child!" he told her. "And all you want to do is sit up in this tower, designing wonderful dresses and fancy suits and shirts. But down on the ground there's a kingdom to run, and I am getting too old to deal with everyone's problems."

The princess wasn't listening. She was too busy working out how best to loop the sash on the dress she was drawing. "What problems?" was all she muttered.

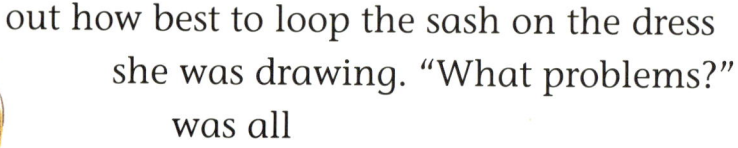

"*What* problems?" The king sighed. "I have told you a thousand times!

Each day brings more bad news about these two giants who are stealing the farmers' sheep for their suppers and uprooting trees for their firewood."

"I have an idea," said the princess. "Send out a Royal Decree. Give a reward to whoever gets rid of the giants. Offer half of the kingdom, then lots of people will want to have a go. Whoever succeeds will be the right one to deal with all the problems you keep talking about."

"May I throw in your hand in marriage?" begged the king.

"No, you may not," said the princess, and went back to fretting about whether the sash should lie softly around the waist of the dress, or hang from the shoulder. (She would have made the sash and held it up to see, but she was dreadful at sewing. Just *dreadful*.)

The king's secretary pinned up the Royal Decree just as the tailor came into the courtyard. He stood and read it.

Wanted

A brave and valiant person to rid the land of two most troublesome giants.

Reward

Half the kingdom.

The tailor was delighted. "This is a task for me!" he told himself. "If I can kill seven at one blow, I can kill two troublesome giants." He told the secretary, "You can take down that notice right now. I'll get the job done today."

The king's secretary stared down his nose at the little tailor. "Oh, yes?" he said sarcastically. "You and whose army?"

But the brave little tailor had already set off back towards the forest to find the two troublesome giants.

Chapter 6

The tailor felt perfectly confident as he walked through the forest. Each time he saw a stone on the path in front of him, he picked it up and put it in his pocket. "If I can throw anything so high it never comes back to Earth, then I can surely throw a stone so hard a giant will fall down dead."

He came upon a line of broken bushes. Guessing that the giants had brushed past them, he followed a trail of squashed bluebells till he stumbled upon the giants taking a nap under the trees.

They were, he saw, the very same two giants that he'd met the night before.

"It would be rude to kill two giants who were so kind to me," he said to himself. "They fed me, and gave me shelter. I will offer them the chance to leave this kingdom peacefully. Only if they refuse will I have no choice but to attack them."

The sight of the giants sleeping so soundly made the little tailor feel tired too. "I'll take a nap as well, until they wake," he told himself. "Although I'd be foolish to lie beside them, in case they roll over and squash me."

He looked around, then up. "There's a fork in the branch of that tree. I could sleep there as comfortably as in a cradle."

He climbed the tree and, since he'd been walking all morning and half of the afternoon, soon fell into the deepest sleep.

Alas, the fork in the branch wasn't as cosy and comfortable as he'd imagined. The tailor tossed and turned as he dreamed, and every time he rolled over, a stone dropped out of his pocket on to the giant beneath.

"Ouch!" cried the giant, waking. He shook his friend's shoulder. "Why did you throw that stone at me?"

"Nonsense!" the other sleepily replied. "I did no such thing."

They settled down again, just as the tailor rolled over once more. Another stone fell on the giant.

"Liar!" he cried. "You've done it again!"

"Not I," said his friend. "I've done nothing except go back to sleep."

Once more, the two of them settled into their dreams. The little tailor rolled over and a third stone fell.

"Ouch!" cried the giant. He warned his friend, "Do that once more and I will teach you a lesson you won't forget in a hurry!"

"Hush!" snapped the other. "You're disturbing my nap."

One last stone fell. "YEE-OW!" cried the giant. Furious, he leaped to his feet, and breaking off a nearby branch, started to hit his friend with it.

"So, that's your game, is it?" cried the other giant. "We shall see who wins this battle!"

And while the little tailor slept overhead, the two angry giants beat one another with branches until both of them lay dead.

Chapter 7

It was more than an hour before the tailor woke and climbed down the tree. There, on the ground before him, lay the giants, both dead as doornails.

At first he was puzzled. But when he looked at his belt, he asked himself, "Why should I be surprised? A man who can kill seven at one blow awake can surely kill two in his sleep!" Proudly, he set off back to the palace, to tell of the very brave thing he had done, and claim half of the kingdom.

At first, no one believed him. A dozen soldiers were sent into the forest to check that he wasn't telling lies, but soon they came back with the news. "Yes, indeed! Both of the troublesome giants lie stone dead."

The king was told, and he immediately invited the little tailor into the throne room. He stared at the tailor for a while, then turned to his daughter, and whispered,

"Does this fellow look to you like someone who can run the kingdom for me, now that I am old?"

The king's daughter said, "The kingdom can muddle through very happily by itself. But if this little man is to stay in the palace, he will need finer clothes. I shall go back to my tower room this very minute to design them."

The king sighed. "See?" he said to the tailor. "My daughter thinks of nothing but designing clothes. Sadly, she is not very handy with the needle, so all her grand designs come to nothing."

"Then she has found just the man in me!" boasted the tailor. "For I can cut and sew and pleat and hem, along with the finest in the land."

And so the tailor and the king's daughter spent the whole day, and many days after that, happily designing and making fine clothes together.

"Well, did she marry him?" I hear you ask.

Nobody knows. All that is clear is that the king's daughter was right. Without the two troublesome giants uprooting trees and stealing sheep, the kingdom muddled along quite happily by itself.

The old belt that boasted *'Seven at one blow!'* was soon thrown into a corner and forgotten. But when news drifted back to the village that their own little tailor had rid the land of two troublesome giants, and now lived in the palace in high style, the jam seller and her friends all scratched their heads. "How very strange," they said to one another. "Could he have been a lot less foolish than we all imagined? A good deal braver than we thought?"

He certainly was *lucky*.

Now answer the questions …

1 How many spoonfuls of jam did the tailor ask to be put in his bowl?

2 Why did the village folk run away giggling, after they saw what the tailor had carved on to his belt?

3 How could you tell that the two giants the tailor met were the same two that were causing trouble for the king?

4 What does the word 'sarcastically' mean on page 24?

5 After reading Chapter 1, did you think it was likely that the tailor would eventually live in a palace?

6 Why do you think the author says it would frighten her to describe the giant's teeth on page 17? What do you think they look like?

7 Is the character of the princess like anyone you know? Would they have acted like the princess if they were supposed to help run a kingdom?

8 Have you read any other stories where somebody makes mistakes, but still receives a reward?